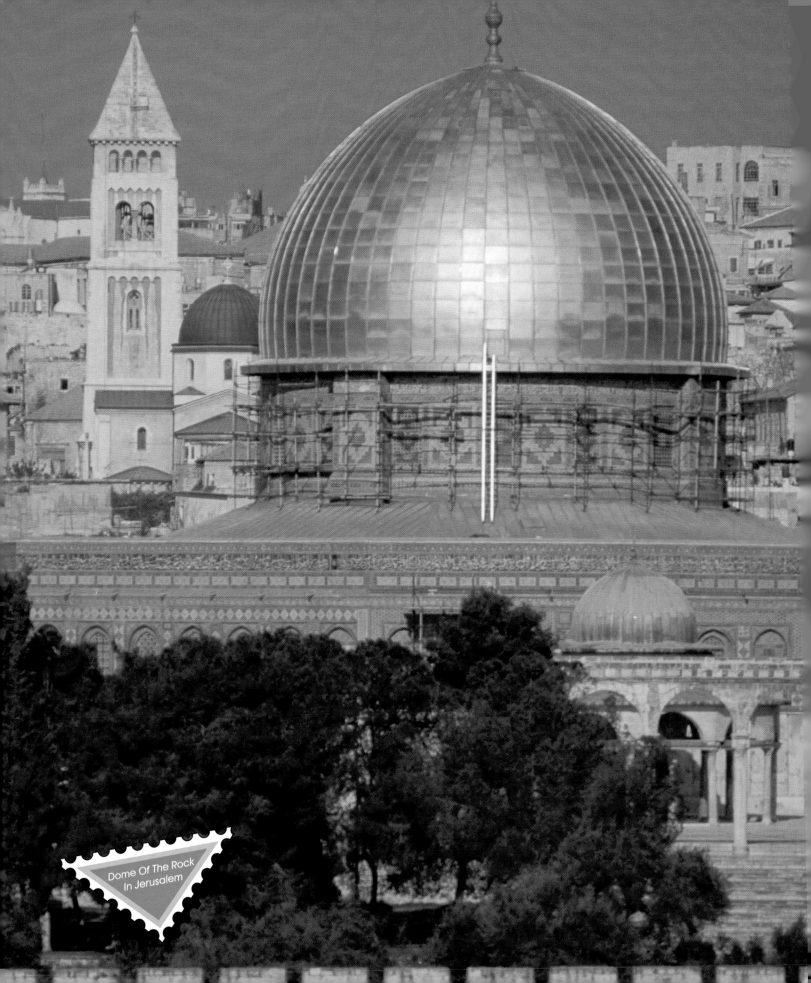

Dome Of The Rock
In Jerusalem

FACES
AND
PLACES

# ISRAEL

BY ELMA SCHEMENAUER

THE CHILD'S WORLD®, INC.

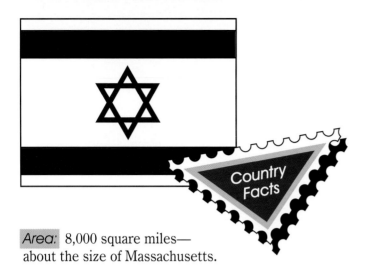

**Country Facts**

*Area:* 8,000 square miles—about the size of Massachusetts.

*Population:* About 6 million people.

*Capital City:* Jerusalem.

*Other Important Cities:* Tel Aviv, Haifa, and Eilat.

*Money:* The New Israeli Shekel (NIS). A New Israeli Shekel is divided into 100 new agorot.

*National Flag:* A white flag with two blue horizontal stripes. It looks like a Hebrew prayer shawl. Between the stripes is a blue star with six points.

*National Song:* "Hatikvah," or "The Hope."

*National Holiday:* Independence Day. It sometimes comes in April and sometimes in May. On the Jewish calendar, it is Iyar 5.

*Head of Government:* The prime minister of Israel.

Text copyright © 2000 by The Child's World®, Inc.
All rights reserved. No part of this book may be reproduced or utilized in any form or by any means without written permission from the publisher.
Printed in the United States of America.

Library of Congress Cataloging-in-Publication Data
Schemenauer, Elma.
Israel / by Elma Schemenauer
Series: "Faces and Places".
p. cm.
Includes index.
Summary: Describes the geography, plants and animals, history, people and culture of Israel.
ISBN 1-56766-600-0 (library : reinforced : alk. paper)

1. Israel — Juvenile literature.
[1. Israel]  I. Title.

DS126.5.S284 1999                    98-45680
956.94 — dc21                              CIP
                                                    AC

**GRAPHIC DESIGN**
Robert A. Honey, Seattle

**PHOTO RESEARCH**
James R. Rothaus / James R. Rothaus & Associates

**ELECTRONIC PRE-PRESS PRODUCTION**
Robert E. Bonaker / Graphic Design & Consulting Co.

**PHOTOGRAPHY**
Cover photo: A young boy participates in Passover Prayer in Jerusalem by Paul A. Souders/Corbis

# Table of Contents

# Where Is Israel?

Imagine you are on a spacecraft looking down at the planet Earth. You would see huge land areas with water around them. These land areas are called **continents**. Some continents are made up of several different countries. Israel is a small country on the continent of Asia.

Israel is in an area of the world called the **Middle East**. Other countries in the Middle East include Egypt, Jordan, Syria, and Lebanon. Israel's borders have often changed because Israel and the other countries in the Middle East want control of certain areas.

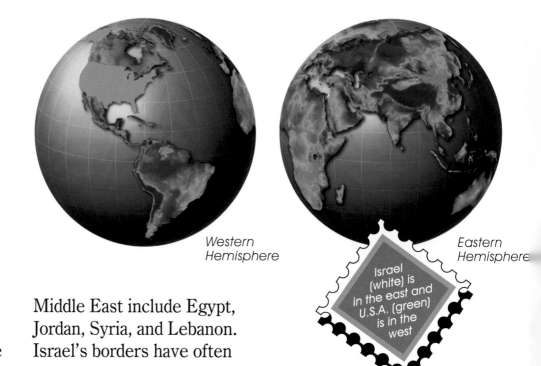

*Western Hemisphere*

*Eastern Hemisphere*

Israel (white) is in the east and U.S.A. (green) is in the west

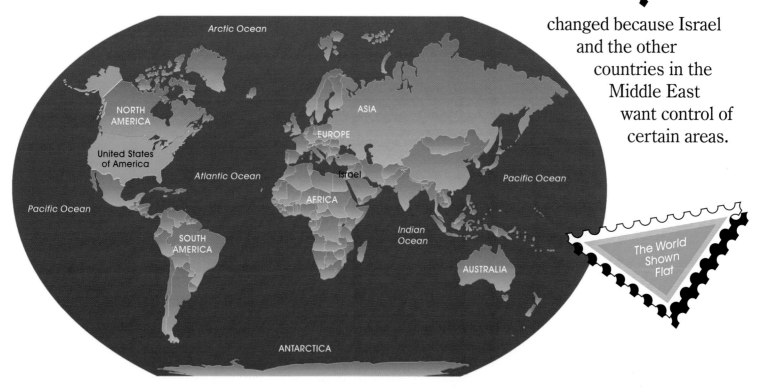

Arctic Ocean

NORTH AMERICA

United States of America

ASIA

EUROPE

Israel

Atlantic Ocean

Pacific Ocean

Pacific Ocean

AFRICA

Indian Ocean

SOUTH AMERICA

AUSTRALIA

ANTARCTICA

The World Shown Flat

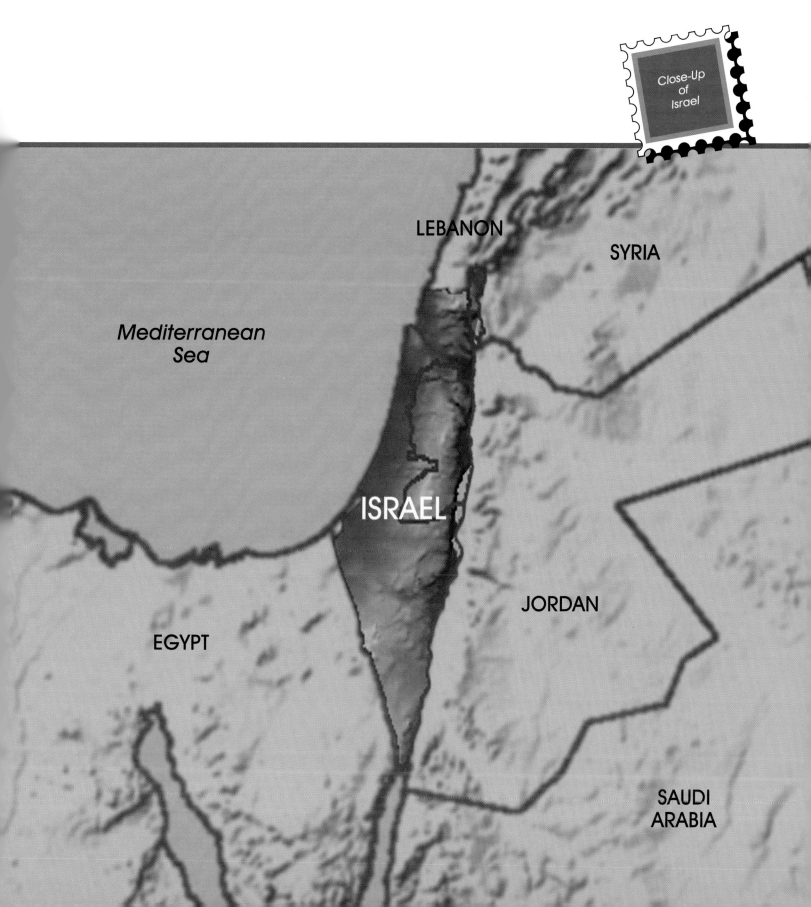

Close-Up
of
Israel

LEBANON

SYRIA

Mediterranean
Sea

ISRAEL

JORDAN

EGYPT

SAUDI
ARABIA

Ramon
Crater
In
Negev
Desert

Mediterranean Sea

Lake Kinneret
(Sea of Galilee)

Jordan
River

Jerusalem ☆

Dead Sea

NEGEV
DESERT

Ramon Crater ■

■ Timna Valley

Shai Ginott/Corbis

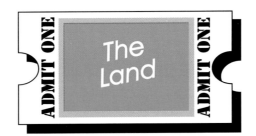

# The Land

Israel's land is in three main strips. Along its Mediterranean coast, the coastal plain can be found. Towards the middle of Israel lies a strip of hills. In the south these hills include the *Negev*, a very dry area that covers about half the country. Inland from the hills is the Jordan River valley.

The *Jordan River* flows from north to south. It connects Israel's only two bodies of water. One of these is the *Sea of Galilee*, or *Lake Kinneret*. The other body of water is the *Dead Sea*, which contains the world's saltiest water.

Solomon's Pillars In Timna Valley

Hanan Isachar/Corbis

The Dead Sea Is 1,296 Feet Below Sea Level, Lowest Place On Earth

The Purcell Team/Corbis

Lake Kinneret (Sea of Galilee)

Richard T. Nowitz/Corbis

# Plants & Animals

Much of Israel was once covered with trees. Most of the trees were cleared away long ago for farming, sheep herding, and cities. But in the last 100 years, people have planted millions of new trees in Israel. They include oak, eucalyptus, and pine. Israel's deserts are too dry to grow trees well. But the deserts have a few freshwater springs. Around these grow lotus trees, reeds, and other plants.

Among Israel's wild animals are foxes, hyenas, jackals, wild pigs, and antelopes. Eagles, hawks, and other birds sail through the air. When *European storks* fly south to Africa for the winter, Israel is on their way. Many storks stop to rest in Israel before continuing on their long journey.

Date Palms Planted In The Negev Desert

Richard T. Nowitz/Corbis

Blanford's Fox In En Gedi Nature Park

Addax In Hai Bar Nature Reserve

Steve Kaufman/Corbis

Steve Kaufman/Corbis

Lake Kinneret
(Sea of Galilee)

En Gedi Nature Park ▪

NEGEV
DESERT

▪ Hai Bar Nature Reserve

Shai Ginott/Corbis

Storks Near
Lake Kinneret

Fortress Of
Masada
Where Zealots
Held Off
The Romans
Until 66 A.D.

Dome of the Rock
Jerusalem ☆
Masada
Nebi Musa
Qumran
Dead Sea

Nathan Benn/Corbis

Much of Israel's history is in the *Bible*. It says that a man named Abraham believed not in many gods, but in one God. Abraham's God promised him a new land, led him to this land (Israel), and made him the father of a new people called the **Israelites**. In time, lack of food forced the Israelites into Egypt. They suffered there for many years as slaves. Finally a man named *Moses* led the Israelites back to Israel, where they lived happily.

Over the years, the Israelites, or **Jews**, had kings of their own. But soon other groups and kingdoms took over. The *Romans* were one group that ruled over the Jews for many years. The Romans destroyed the Jews' temple and their capital, Jerusalem. The Jews scattered to other countries. But in the late 1800s, Jews from Russia and other lands started coming back to Israel to live.

The Dead Sea Scrolls Were Found In These Qumran Caves

Richard T. Nowitz/Corbis

Ted Spiegel/Corbis

Dome Of The Rock, Muslims Believe Muhammed Rose To Heaven From The Rock

Jews Believe The Rock Is Where Abraham Was Ordered To Sacrifice Isaac

Nebi Musa Where Some Believe Moses And Muhammed's Wife Are Buried

Richard T. Nowitz/Corbis

# Israel Today

When the Jews began returning to Israel, it had a different name—Palestine. People called **Arabs** lived there. As Jewish newcomers settled in Palestine, fighting began. The Arabs did not want the Jews in Palestine. Other countries learned about the fighting. To bring peace, Palestine was split into two states—one Jewish, the other Arab.

Peter Turnley/Corbis

Soldier Listens To An Unhappy Palestinian From Ramallah

The Palestinian Arabs and neighboring countries did not like this decision. In the war that followed, Israel gained more land, and other countries took over most of Palestine's Arab state. This made the Palestinian Arabs even MORE angry. Ever since, there has been a lot of fighting between Israel and the Palestinians. There have also been fights between Israel and its neighbors.

Israeli Soldiers At Rest In Sinai, 1972

David Rubinger/Corbis

Buddy Mays/Corbis

Ancient, And Mostly Arab, City Of David

Jerusalem ☆ •Ramallah
City of David

SINAI

Sadat (Egypt), Carter (U.S.A.) And Begin (Israel), Signed 1979 Peace Treaty

Wally McNamee/Corbis

Sephardic Jews From Jerusalem Having A Picnic

Nazareth •

Wailing Wall
Jerusalem ☆
Bethlehem •

Annie Griffiths Belt/Corbis

# The People

Israel is the only country in the world in which most of the people are Jews. Israel's European Jews are called *Ashkenazim*. Its Asian and African Jews are called *Sephardim*. Jews born in Israel are called *Sabra*, after a cactus fruit that is prickly on the outside but sweet on the inside. Some say that is how the people are, too!

The rest of Israel's people are mainly Palestinian Arabs. Unlike the Jews, who practice the Jewish faith, most Palestinian Arabs belong to the Muslim religion.

Dave Bartruff/Corbis

A Palestinian Arab From Bethlehem

Orthodox Jews At The Wailing Wall

Arab Man And Sabra Lady Buying Tomatoes In Nazareth

Daniel Lainé/Corbis

Gary Braasch/Corbis

# City Life And Country Life

Most Israelis live in cities. The cities are often big, with tall buildings and crowded streets. A city family usually buys an apartment in which to live. On the edges of cities, some families live in houses.

In the country, an Israeli family may live in a special kind of village called a **kibbutz**. Instead of farming for money or food, Kibbutz members raise crops for the whole community.

When kibbutzim started in the early 1900s, many were in dry or dangerous areas. By sharing the crops they raised, every Kibbutz member got enough to eat—even if their own area did not grow very well! Besides kibbutzim, Israel has several other kinds of country villages.

Townhouses In Acre Built With Government Money

David H. Wells/Corbis

Farming On A Kibbutz In The Negev Desert

Seaside Apartments In Yafo

Hanan Isachar/Corbis

Richard T. Nowitz/Corbis

Acre

Yafo
Jerusalem ☆

*NEGEV
DESERT*

Paul A. Souders/Corbis

Hillside
Apartments
In
Jerusalem

Muslim
Girl In
Computer
Programming
Class At
Umm el Fahm

GOLAN HEIGHTS

•Umm el Fahm

Jerusalem ☆

In Israel, children must go to school until they are 16 years old. There are separate schools for Jews and Arabs. Besides the usual school subjects, Jewish children study the Bible, Jewish faith, and Jewish culture. Arab children study a holy book called the *Koran* and Muslim faith and culture.

Hebrew and Arabic are Israel's main languages. Jewish schools use Hebrew, but students may study Arabic if they wish. Arabic schools use Arabic, but students also study Hebrew starting in the fourth grade. Because people from many different countries have moved to Israel, many other languages are spoken, too. English is one language that many children learn in school. Russian has also become a common language in Israel.

Young Girl In Computer Class In Jerusalem

Nik Wheeler/Corbis

Israeli Teacher Instructing Boys In The Golan Heights

Paul A. Souders/Corbis

Jewish Sacred Torah Scrolls

Arab Holy Book The Koran

Richard T. Nowitz/Corbis

Bojan Brecelj/Corbis

## Work

Cleaning Solar Engery Panels In The Negev Desert

Richard T. Nowitz/Corbis

Israelis are very smart and skilled. They make computers, books, medical equipment, and medicines. Many others have skills to cut diamonds in beautiful ways. In fact, Israel leads the world in diamond cutting and polishing—even though it has no diamonds of its own! Israel must bring diamonds in from other lands.

Israel is a hot, dry land. Even so, Israelis make the most of what they have. They get table salt and other minerals from the Dead Sea. They carefully use the little water they have to grow cotton, barley, wheat, almonds, vegetables, and fruit, especially oranges and grapefruit. In some places, Israelis use sunshine to make electricity. Plenty of sunshine is one thing Israel has!

David Rubinger/Corbis

Bedouin Market Worker In Beersheba

Diamond Cutter From Ramat Gan

Nik Wheeler/Corbis

Ramat Gan

Dead Sea

Beersheba

NEGEV
DESERT

Iddan

This Mango
Grove Near
Iddan Is
Irrigated
With Salt
Water

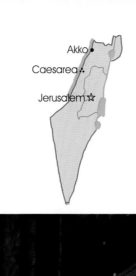

Akko •
Caesarea ⁘
Jerusalem ☆

Outdoor
Nachat
Shiva
Cafes In
Jerusalem

# Food

Like their Middle Eastern neighbors, Israelis enjoy lamb, rice, eggplant, pita bread, and a sesame seed paste called **tahini**. Israel's European Jews have introduced other dishes, too. These include chicken soup, chopped liver, borscht (beet soup), and latkes (potato fritters). Israel, land of many peoples, also has dishes ranging from Vietnamese egg rolls to American hamburgers.

Bedouin Woman Bakes Pita Bread

Shai Ginott/Corbis

Kosher Buffet In Caesarea

Plates Of Arab Appetizers From Akko

Dave Bartruff/Corbis

Nik Wheeler/Corbis

# Pastimes

Israelis have fun in many of the same ways Americans do. They especially like to read, go to concerts, and watch their basketball and soccer teams on TV. At the Dead Sea, people love to float on the thick, salty water. It won't let them sink, even if they can't swim.

Richard T. Nowitz/Corbis

Laying On The Water Of The Dead Sea

Israel has a number of events for large groups of people. One is the yearly Jerusalem March, during which thousands of Israelis and non-Israelis walk together to Israel's capital city, Jerusalem. Other events include marathons for runners. Every four years Israel holds the Maccabiah Games for Jewish athletes from around the world. Israeli athletes also compete in the Olympics.

Richard T. Nowitz/Corbis

Riding Camels In Desert Near Eilat

Friends Wading By Falls In En Gedi Nature Park

Morton Beebe, S.F./Corbis

Jerusalem ☆
Bet Guvrin National Park ■      Dead Sea
■ En Gedi Nature Park

● Eilat

Richard T. Nowitz/Corbis

Tel Aviv
Jerusalem
Dome of the Rock ☆
Holocaust Museum

Paul A. Souders/Corbis

Rabbi
Blowing
Shofar
For Passover
In Jerusalem

# Holidays

**ADMIT ONE** · **ADMIT ONE**

For everyday life, Israelis use the same calendar most Americans do. But for holidays, Jewish Israelis use the Jewish calendar. One Jewish holiday is *Passover*. During Passover, Jews thank God for bringing them out of Egypt. Israel's Muslims, who are mostly Arabs, have their own calendar, too. They use it for Muslim holidays. One is *'Id-al-Adha*, when Muslims celebrate Abraham's strong faith in God. Israel's Christians celebrate their own holidays, including Christmas and Easter.

Israel is a very important country. Two of the world's religions (Christianity and the Jewish faith) started there. Israel is also important to the Muslim religion. Israel is a good place to learn about these three religions. It is also an interesting place to visit. Every year, thousands of visitors travel to Israel— not only to learn about religions, but to have fun in the sun, too!

Moshe Shai/Corbis

Child Dressed For The Adloyda Festival In Tel Aviv

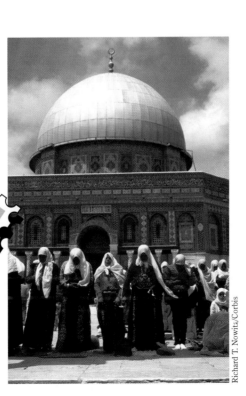

Muslim Women At Dome Of The Rock Celebrate Abrahams Faith In God

Richard T. Nowitz/Corbis

Relief
Sculpture
At
Holocaust
Museum

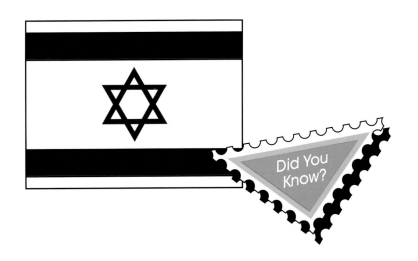

Did You Know?

Israelis have a long history, but their country is quite young. Israel celebrated its 50th birthday in 1998.

Israeli postage stamps and coins are in three languages— Hebrew, Arabic, and English.

The Hebrew word for both hello and goodbye is the same. It is "shalom," which means "peace."

The Jewish religion has strict rules about food. Only certain animals may be eaten as food. Meat and milk products may not be eaten at the same meal, either. Many Israelis are careful to follow these rules.

How Do You Say?

|  | HEBREW | HOW TO SAY IT |
|---|---|---|
| Hello | shalom | (sha–LOHM) |
| Goodbye | shalom | (sha–LOHM) |
| Please | b'vakasha | (b'vah–kah–shah) |
| Thank You | toda | (toh–dah) |
| One | ahat | (ah–haht) |
| Two | shtayim | (sh'tah–yim) |
| Three | shalosh | (shah–losh) |
| Israel | Yisrael | (YISS–rah–ell) |

## Glossary

**Arabs (AIR–abs)**
Arabs are a group of people who live in the Middle East. Many Arabs live in Palestine.

**continents (KON–tih–nents)**
Most of the land areas on Earth are divided up into big sections called continents. Israel is on the continent of Asia.

**Israelites (IZ–ray–el–lites)**
The Israelites were the people of the first kingdom of Israel. When food got scarce, the Israelites had to leave Israel and flee to Egypt.

**Jews (JOOZ)**
Jews are people who belong to the Jewish religion. Most of Israel's people are Jews.

**kibbutz (kih–BUUTZ)**
A kibbutz is a farm or settlement where people work together. On a kibbutz, people share the crops they grow and the things they make.

**Middle East (MIH–dull EEST)**
The Middle East is an area of the world that includes such countries as Egypt, Syria, Lebanon, Jordan, and Kuwait. Israel lies in the Middle East.

**tahini (tah–HEE–nee)**
Tahini is a smooth paste made from sesame seeds. Many Israelis like to eat tahini.

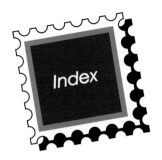

## Index